The Frustrated Carer

By Brianne George

Illustrated by John Elson

The Frustrated Carer by Brianne George.
Published by Brianne George
Website: www.briannegeorge.co.uk

Illustrations by John Elson

Printed in Great Britain by Amazon

ISBN: 978-1-7396471-1-7

Edition One

Disclaimer

** Warning: This book contains mature and what can be seen as offensive language**

This book is a memoir. It reflects the author's present recollections of experiences over time. Names and characteristics have been changed, events and places have been compressed and dialogue has been re-created.

The contents of this book are based on personal experiences of Brianne George and her life and her encounters as an unpaid carer. It is not intended to offend but to highlight her encounters within the social care system. All Views and opinions are that of the author.

Facts are correct at time of writing.

Dedication

This book is dedicated to my mum, dad and daughter as well as paid and unpaid carers in the UK, without whom, I would never have experienced the wonderful, crazy, frustrating, world of caring.

Thank yous

I would also like to thank my fellow friends and family, who I have turned to for editorial checks and feedback of the contents ahead of launch.

Index

Welcome From Brianne George

Hi there,

I am Brianne George. First of all, a huge thank you for picking up this book to read. I hope you have a few giggles and laughs along the way, with some light bulb moments of, 'oh yes I have been there!' Or maybe it will act as an eye opener of how the world can be viewed from a carer's eyes.

I felt compelled to release this book for publication after I had many paid carers laughing at my predicament and my 'can you believe this happened?' daily unleashing onto them as they walked through the door.

As some of the carers turned into friends, or indeed were friends to start with, one carer who came through our door said to me, "I would never believe this, had I not lived it with you!'

So, after another frustrating episode with the authorities, I thought, 'it's like hitting your head against a brick wall' ... and my head was sore. This caused me to unleash into this book, which is based on my experiences of the care system, and I really hope you can find yourself a small piece of time to put your feet up and come in to my world for a minute or two. Please remember, us unpaid carers are not frustrated all the time, we do laugh and we do see the funny side of situations, because if you don't you would cry.

Caring: An Overview

Oh, for goodness' sake,

This book that I have tried to make,

Has driven me nuts for crying out loud,

Just so it might stand out in the crowd.

Then me editor starts shouting at me,

You got to start it as funny as can be,

Grab the attention of your reader in the first paragraph,

It's really important to make them laugh.

Then I have the printers cursing at me,

Keep in the margins or lose them pictures for eternity,

Not to mention me husband the little git,

Calling out, why haven't you finished it?

And in the middle of it all during my care duty today,

I have an hour-long conversation with the man at Age UK,

Then to the loo to look after Auntie Joan,

But as they say you shouldn't moan!

Only joking, I then wouldn't have a book,

How's about it? Want to have a look?

Unfortunately, business comes first,

You have to hold on to quench your humour thirst,

Laying the foundations for those who may not know,

This is why the care system is so full of woe!

So on a serious note a quick lesson for you,

Before we see what those in the care system get up to.

There are two definitions of carers in the UK,

Unpaid carers that do it for love and paid carers that do it for pay,

Some paid carers are fab, whilst the others are not,

Paid carers get paid holiday whilst unpaid carers are forgot.

Whether paid or not, there can be a frustration you share,

When you look after those whose lives have become too hard to bear,

Someone, somewhere that finds everyday living hard,

They may have been a doctor, a lawyer or a writer of a

birthday card.

They could have been a paid carer, a nurse, a cleaner, who

knows,

But with illness and disability sometimes the struggle

shows,

They could be a child, a teenager or an adult,

And unpaid carers and family on their knees is not the

disabled's fault.

Eventually the family may reach out to get some help in,

Not realising what the paid carers are going through

themselves within,

And by this time unpaid carers can be on the floor,

They need someone who can do more.

Sometimes families are lucky, get a good carer and they strive,

Sometimes they are not, they get a bad carer, and a further burden arrives.

So based on my own experiences and others too,

Here is a selection of my thoughts just for you,

So, please put your feet up and see how many similarities we share,

Between you and I and for those of whom we care.

Unpaid Carers

Unpaid carers are
everywhere,
But you may not realise
they care,

Unpaid carers are
different you see,
They are your friends
and family.

They are the ones who get up in the night,
Without any complaint in sight,
They do not get paid for their deeds,
They are the ones financially in need.

This set of carers have probably gone,
Without a decent wage for far too long,
Their savings have been spent on necessity things,
Like medical equipment and all that disability brings,

The government gives

them £67.50 per week,

To pay the bills and for

their keep,

But to claim you must

give 35-hours a week of

care,

Less than two pounds an hour, that's all they can spare.

These carers give up everything to look after family,

But are met with a whole host of bureaucracy,

'Cause they really love and care, they really do,

They are unselfish, giving and worn-out,

Their love and compassion is not in doubt,

A lot of them are millionaires of love, but money poor,

And when material needs comes knocking at the door,

Where do they turn to? you may say,

I know they benefit scrounge from my taxes all day!

Some look at them as scum of the earth,

Who are too lazy to get a job and haven't worked a day

since birth.

They see them at home all day,

Scrounging for the taxes that workers pay,

They don't realise all the hospitals you attend,

Or the emotional support you give your family or friend.

They don't see the mental state the household is in,

Coping with every little thing,

From feeding to drinking and cutting up food,

Trying your best to lighten the mood.

They don't see the red bureaucratic tape you dance

through,

Just to get a bob or two.

You speak to one person followed by many more,

To get something simple for your cared for,

It might be Attendance Allowance or DLA,

Anything will help to see you OK,

But that only covers necessities,

Not other liabilities!

What happens when the washing machine doesn't start?

You haven't the money, but you have the heart,

And off into the begging stage you go,

To charities who often say 'NO',

'We don't give white goods or washing machines OK,

I suggest you try another agency today'.

You get passed from one to another,

Just so you can wash the urine-soaked sheets of your

brother,

Who like others just hasn't a clue,

Of every little thing you do.

So, to all those who have never been there,

Who think all unpaid carers are treated more than fair,

Karma is wonderful it's true,

Look down your noses and it will catch up with you,

Instead look around you and try to see,

What the scroungers next door cope with as a family,

Don't assume all is ok,

And that they screwed the system for extra pay.

It really is not that easy,

To cut through tape and bureaucracy,

And some carers just don't ask anymore,

Too much bother on top of their chores,

And if you still don't believe it all fits,

Do a job swap with those unpaid carers on benefits,

And to the many who know the unpaid carers worth,

It is good to have your support upon this earth.

Peppercorn Crumbs

Covid has changed things in care,

You want it, but it is not really there,

You finally succumbs,

To accepting Peppercorn Crumbs.

Many unpaid carers will get what I say,

The care agency says no-one today,

Go find someone else to take over these slots,

Because

Peppercorn

Crumbs is all

that we got.

So, you end up thanking them profusely,

For two hours and not twenty-three,

Because at the end of the day you are not dumb,

And you have to accept Peppercorn Crumbs.

The District Nurse

Ah, the district nurses, thank God for them,

They come and visit, time and time again!

They come and say,

How are you doing today?

They take a look at mum and put your mind at rest,

But recently they have lost their Zest,

You can only summise,

Why there is nothing there between their eyes.

They, like us, are

walking on eggshells

too,

Whilst caring and

knowing what to do,

They have been over

run,

With caring for

everyone.

Then they come upon people like me,

Sanitising everything that you can see,

Oh, they have touched the banister on the stair,

Let me spray some sanitiser there.

Oh yes, I have followed them around,

Making sure we are not Covid bound,

Making sure they wash their hands before they touch,

The one that we care for so ruddy much.

You see the district nurses visit lots of people,

Including your loved one me treacle,

You question if they have just seen Ernie down the road,

And if his symptoms tally with the Covid code?

Over-ran with the elderly,

The hospitals send them home to thee,

And no one knows for sure,

If with them, Covid has come over the door.

The professionals will sort it out,

The ones who see everyone no doubt,

Or the carers at the bottom of the tree,

The unpaid carers like you and me!

From giving insulin to palliative care,

For the families they are always there,

Their knowledge of issues has to be vast,

To cope with what they have been cast.

Too many people now you see,

Are heading into the community,

Where district nurses look after them,

Ensuring their safety time and time again.

They risk their lives as they go door to door,

Trying their best, that's for sure,

But not enough nurses to go around,

Leaves a lot of people alone, whilst homeward bound.

Yet for us they would always cheerily say,

'Hey Sandra, how are you today?'

Behind their smile,

Was someone who hasn't stopped for a while.

Imagine going from door to door,

Wondering if today you would catch Covid for sure,

They had to risk their life,

To save another living on the edge of a knife.

Always there for me at my door,

They kept me going that is for sure,

They were people I went to for advice,

But in this pandemic a lot of them paid the price.

Alzheimer's

Alzheimer's, where the brain slowly dies,

The sufferer meets their demise,

The family, they do too,

They go through this with you.

You forget and so do they,

But you live on forever and a day,

And if this is jumbled, what I just said,

Imagine having Alzheimer's living in your head!

The Thief

For years, your loved one, it was plain to see,

Has been an upright pillar of the community,

But dementia comes a knocking,

And the norm it is a blocking,

And to your utter disbelief,

They turn into the local thief!

Or, if they have not thieved it themselves,

They can become receivers of stolen goods upon their

shelves.

Oh yes, you visit your loved one in a community setting,

And you see that presents they are getting,

But where did the necklace come from, that round her

neck she has gained?

You ask everyone around, but no one can explain.

Then Doris in the bed next door,

Walks past her bed holding jewellery galore,

And pauses and looks at your elder for a bit,

Before handing them a golden bracelet,

Your elder with dementia too,

Looks and says a meaning full, "Thank you".

"Look" they says with tears in their eyes,

"I had lost this and she found it to my surprise",

You realise that it does not belong to your elder,

Neither does the dusting powder.

So, you ask a nurse to see what they say,

They reply, "Doris does this every day!"

Then Doris' daughter arrives at her bed,

Looks at the jewellery and shakes her head,

It is no use trying to explain,

That taking others jewellery is not a game.

But those she has thieved off have dementia too,

And they just don't have a clue,

So, relatives spend their visiting time,

Trying to solve their relatives crime,

No one knows who owns the stuff they took,

And your elder has turned into the local crook!

Now Betsy on the other hand,

Her thieving was of a particular brand.

The nurse who ran when an emergency came in,

Left the medicine cabinet open and caused a din,

As a loud cry of "Sweeties" you hear her say,

As you realise that the meds are now her personal buffet!

Oh yes, those lovely pills that you can clearly see,

Are sweeties to the lovely little Betsy!

No one is around with the mental ability to say no,

Other than you, so off to her defence you go.

You guide Betsy from the diazepam buffet,

Another thief on the ward that day!

The truth is the disease of dementia is the real villain,

Changing the view of the world they live in.

The pillar of the community,

Who would never steal from you or me,

Is now a thief,

And it all just beggars belief.

Getting Mum To Eat

Getting mum to eat,

Is no ordinary feat,

The lady who once ate like a king,

Now won't eat a fucking thing!

It starts with breakfast as the sun comes up,

'Mum what can I get you in your coffee cup?'

Silence and a glare is all you get,

Maybe she hasn't woken yet?

You wait five minutes to let her awake,

Before asking again what drink she'd like to take?

Then she shouts 'please stop doing this to me,

I don't want anything! I'm not thirsty!'

'Ok mum so what about something to eat?'

As you sit and quiver on the fitted sheet,

The glare you get sets you straight,

She doesn't want anything on her plate.

'Can I tempt you with a yogurt today?'

But her mouth stays shut she has nothing to say,

'What about some toast? You could have a slice?

Mum if you answered me that would be nice'.

But all you get is that deathly stare,

You think I will get her up and into the chair,

When she's there she may eat for me,

She may even take a cup of tea.

You look at her sat in the chair,

'Can I tempt you with a fresh cream eclair?'

'No thank you' comes the reply,

'But if you don't eat you will die!

What can I get you mum because you haven't eaten today?'

'Oooooooo I have had loads' is all she will say,

'But mum you haven't and I'm worried about you,

You're so thin I don't know what to do.'

'Oh you do lie I am really fat,

You feed me like a Cheshire Cat,

You give me food all day long,

And I have to decline it to stay strong.'

Yep hand on heart I can honestly say,

Getting mum to eat could go on all day!

Eventually off to the doc you go,

Mum is filling me with lots of woe,

I can't get her to eat for me,

No breakfast, lunch or her tea!

So, the doc hands you a tool to use,

A prescription for Fortijuice!

Oh yes, this will feed her as she will drink,

This will do the job you think.

They come in different flavours including Apple,

This is something she won't grapple,

She loves her apple juice does my old mum,

This will have her anorexia overcome!

So, you hand the drink to her,

For breakfast, lunch and Dinner,

You see her come back to life,

You no longer feel on the edge of a knife.

But then a new carer comes over the door,

Who knows just what the Fortijuice is for,

And with a big smile and little to do,

She exclaims 'wow they will put calories on you!'

And with that your efforts have been foiled,

With one comment getting mum to eat has been spoiled,

Your mum pouts as she takes the straw from her lips,

And exclaims 'all these calories on my hips!'

She hands the carton back to you as you say,

'Are you going to eat for me today?'

She shakes her head and says 'no',

Back comes those feelings of woe.

And once again you feel defeat,

Over the battle of getting mum to eat!

Working And Caring

It's eight in the morning,

And once more your workplace is a calling,

Your hair and make-up is all done,

Just waiting for the agency to come and look after your

loved one,

But as that clock ticks, they are nowhere in sight,

So, you are now in the middle of a work/home crazy fight.

You cannot leave your loved one alone,

But you need money for the bills and mortgage you own,

You pace up and down whilst your loved one needs care,

But how to go to work when the agency is not there?

You call into work and try to explain,

The agency has not turned up again,

And eventually work can put up with this no more,

And you lose your security as you are booted out of the

door.

You Have A Pad On!

The elderly, sat on a ward all day,

Will often call out and you will hear them say,

"Can you

take me

to the

toilet

my

dear?"

'But you have a pad on!' is all you will hear,

With no help from the nurse to pee in privacy,

They use their pads to have a wee,

But worse still and what a to do,

The same is said for a number two.

Well, your brain whizzes round and you cannot believe
what you hear,
And you know you can do better for one so dear,
You decide, I'm taking them home with me,
Where they can pee in privacy!

Oh yes! You can do better than they,
And you take your elder home to stay!
Into the spare bed they can go,
I can cope with this small woe.

I will take them to the toilet when they need a wee,
It's easy, you just wait and see!
I will take them every two hours,
Much better than hospital, this place of ours.

Now, what it is that you did not see,
Is mum shuffling on her way to pee,
Half an hour later you are still in the hall,
Wondering if you will get to the toilet at all?

'Mum, can't you
move faster?'
you calmly
seethe,

But mum says,
'I'm going fast,
I just can't
breathe!'

You think this is just a blip for her,
You will get her on the toilet you concur,
Eventually mum makes it to the loo,
But with the effort you sit down too.

Now it comes for time for her to wipe her bum,
She can do this your old mum,
As the toilet tissue in the air appears,
What she does next can leave you in tears.

'Mum wipe your bottom please, you know what to do',

But she wipes her nose whilst sat on the loo,

'Um mum, that's not your bottom, that's your nose,

You know where the toilet paper goes'.

'Will you be quiet?' she shouts at you,

'I know that! I'm going to the loo.'

So, you leave her a while to do her thing,

Sat outside on the landing.

'Are you finished yet Mum? you have been a while,'

You call through to her feeling vile,

We wouldn't like it if someone sat outside the bathroom
door,

Asking if we were doing some more.

You toilet in peace, that's what you were brought up to do,

Not having someone watch over you,

With no word coming back, you go inside,

And there she is with a bare backside,

Trying to stand up in her own unique way,

With teeth a missing and her hair all grey.

So, you steady her to her feet,

This is not an easy feat!

As mum stretches her hand out to yours,

You take her weight, so she doesn't face-plant the floor.

Your aim is to help her slowly back to her chair,

Things will be easier once she gets there,

But you remember the time she took to get to pee,

And you know walking back isn't going to be easy.

So, you grab a wheelchair and push her back,

'I can walk' she shouts and gives you flack,

'Yes, but mum I have dinner to cook,

And it's now seven o clock - Look!

You started this lark an hour ago,

Not realising it would cause so much woe,

You show her your watch but she can't see,

She struggles to read for eternity.

'Never mind Mum' you shout in her ear,

Shouting because she just can't hear,

Or she has selective hearing some may say,

You just want her back to her chair either way.

After much persuasion you get her to use the gadget with
wheels,

So, you can get into the kitchen to prepare the family
meals,

Now getting her out the other end,

This is not easy my fellow friend.

Because now she refuses to get out of her wheels that you
gave to her,

In fact she is refusing and it's causing a stir!

Eventually with a grin and a pain in your back,

You get her into the chair with even more verbal flack.

BUT you don't give in you think she will get well,

And this was just a one-off kind of hell,

The days pass by and you struggle through,

Giving mum her dignity whilst she does a poo.

No more mum sitting in a soiled, dirty pad,

You can do this, it's hard but you are glad,

But, one day turns to three
then four,

The toilet trips start to get
you at the core.

Going to the toilet that takes you,

A minute to do,

Is a totally different ball game,

When the mental health of the elderly is in the frame.

Eventually, you reach for the phone and call,

A care agency to deal with it all,

But for some reason or another,

You still have to deal with your mother.

The agency cannot be there all the time,

And mums bowel habits have no reason or rhyme,

Whilst paid carers are there for an hour or two,

During that time mum may not want the loo.

So you still have to deal with toileting every day,

When eventually, you yourself have to say,

The famous words the nurses said all day long,

No toilet. You got a pad on!

And so it starts the changing of pads,

They would do it for us - our mums and dads.

And the guilt that builds up inside,

Because you've taken mums dignity and pride.

But the truth is it's

her or you,

You are knackered

because of trips to

the loo.

By the time she gets there,

And back to her chair,

An hour is gone,

It may not appear too long,

But when you do that four or five times a day,

Your world is overtaken and your full of dismay!

Then mums constipation, you deal with that too,

Oh yes - the doc gives laxatives so she can do a poo,

But you know folks what is coming I'm sure,

That pad that was holding it, holds it no more!

It's down her leg and all smelly and rank,

It's in her pad and up her flank,

She has no idea what she has just done,

Not with the mental health of your old mum.

But what is staring you right in the eyes,

Over her buttocks and over her thighs,

Is that the only person present to clear away this poo,

Is the one and only YOU!!

So, on go the gloves and apron and smile,

You get her onto her bed for a while,

You change her like the baby you once were,

It's now your time to do it for her.

As you go through baby wipes one after another,

Whilst smiling sweetly, under your breath, you are cursing

at mother,

Who is this person that you have become?

You are not my hygienic, caring mum!

But you get her clean with bum in your face,

Putting a clean pad back in place,

You change all her clothes, so she smells nice once more,

And pray to God there's no more poo in store.

Caring for the elderly with an incontinence need,

Brings a lot of challenges indeed,

You can train them again to use the toilet,

But time-consuming toileting is what you will get.

Or you learn from the nurses that so angered you,

Because they wouldn't take mum to the loo,

And you use the pads that sometimes you get for free,

From the district nurses and the local OT,

And when you finally go to bed at night,

You know another day of

pads and pee is in sight.

But we do not put ourselves ahead of others,

So we can look after our fathers and mothers.

A Short One

Just a quick little poem for you to read,

Yep, a very short one indeed,

That's it! That is all you have time for,

Your loved one needs you, need I say more?

My Neighbour Next Door

My neighbour next door,

She is a 'cared for',

Her carers arrive on time each day,

But she can't understand a word they say.

Her daughter tells me they can't read,

She leaves them notes that they don't heed,

'Please put stairlift upstairs when you are done,

She falls over it does my elderly mum'.

Then when they come in later that day,

The house is in disarray,

And why? Because Mrs. is on the floor,

And they are here for her, the cared for.

Now, if they had put the stairlift upstairs as asked,

My mother wouldn't be sat there on her arse!

And you would not have to call for someone to help you,

Get mum off the floor in an hour or two!

To do just one thing would have saved all of this,

But Common Sense and reading appears amiss!

The Housing Scoop

Have you ever broken your leg and not been able to move?

Have you ever broken an arm and really lost you groove?

Has this then had an effect on how you live your life?

Maybe you couldn't get up the stairs, and had to depend on the wife?

Maybe you just did not go to bed as it was easier to sleep downstairs?

Now imagine if that was permanent, let's see how life then compares?

For up and down this country, thousands are permanently sat,

In their living room and permanent poor mobility has caused that,

Oh no, they cannot go upstairs to use the toilet you know,

They have to use a commode in the living room when they want to go,

And what about going to bed at night,

Getting up them stairs is too much of a fight.

So, with duvets and pillows handed to them, they sleep downstairs,

This can cause issues and unseen housing nightmares,

What about a shower to make them nice and clean?

They cannot get upstairs to make themselves glean,

So, they have a strip wash and hope that this will do,

But overtime this doesn't get them as clean as me or you!

For you are so lucky to have all those limbs that work for now,

You do not have to work out, how to get upstairs somehow,

You do not have to eat in the same room as you poop,

Therefore, these people have no choice but to go on the housing scoop!

Oh, the good old housing situation is a nightmare if you lose your groove,

You see, for the disabled, it is bloody diabolical if they have to move!

Adaptions are usually not allowed in private rented property,
So disabled tenants are living in adaption poverty.

For those who own their own houses, who are now skint and poor,
They have a whole host of crap to get adaptions at their door,
Don't think the mortgage companies will lend a penny to them,
They are on benefits now and can't up the mortgage again.

In fact, they will not reduce it and allow them to move,
A disabled facilities grant is the only way to have their situation improve,
Many disabled may go to them lovely chaps in town,
Them Estate agents, that take away this disability frown,
But my friends, they will probably laugh them out the door,
'What take on housing benefit? That's not who we are here for!'

Off to the council they will go and say,

I hear you help disabled folk, and have houses to give

away,

'Oh, I can see the predicament, and we would love to help

for sure,

But there is already a queue, going out the door.

Then they will say the usual norm,

'ere you are, fill out this form.'

So, off they toddle with their ten-page form in hand,

Cancelling everything that today they had planned,

And fill out the form as best they can,

And hand it back to the council man.

Then they send the form to their good old doc,

Whilst the disabled are living in the lounge round the

clock,

It takes MONTHS for all this to go through,

With no thought about the disabled and their portable loo.

It is not just one person, living in this way,

Too many on a list, to get this type of housing today.

And the rigmarole that one has to go through you would

never believe,

And to get the right property is just so hard to achieve.

So, my friends, next time you run upstairs to do your daily

poop,

Remember our friends out there that are in the housing

Scoop!

Paying For Care

As I grew up money I had,

They had made it, my mum and dad,

I assumed everyone had enough money to live,

Because time to work they did give.

How wrong I was to think this way,

Just because you work night and day,

Does not mean that you are financially secure,

And that you will never have debt knocking at your door.

50 years on with experience under my belt,

Now I know how others have felt,

The truth of course is that it's true,

If you are financially secure, it is easier to do,

You are not told who you can get in to help with care,

You can get who you want with piles of money sitting

there.

BUT when it is off to the state you go,

Unless you are lucky you can be left full of woe.

For at this end of the scale you get,

Unpaid carers struggling with a load of debt.

Unpaid Carers get less than minimum wage whilst the agencies take a mint,

Leaving unpaid carers really skint.

But with money in the bank you can just buy what is needed,

Not so many forms to fill or so many rules to be heeded.

This cuts your workload in half, so you have TIME to actually care,

For those who need you to physically be there.

With money in the bank, you can get experienced carers and be merry,

Unlike agencies who advertise 'no experience necessary'!

With anything from a morning to two weeks training in tow,

They are now qualified to look after Aunty Flo,

They think they are now a walking encyclopedia, but they are NOT,

You get unexperienced and untrained carers, that's what you have got!

I don't blame the paid carers or the agencies who try their best,

Many paid Carers have just lost their zest,

They are leaving the sector in their droves,

To earn more money stacking loaves.

The agencies are desperate for anyone at all,

'No experience necessary' is what they call,

So, then instability and uncaring attitudes creep in,

Because the answer does not lie with agencies but with the system.

But with plenty of money sat there,

You get a choice of how to care.

His garden needs sorting out,

So, you lift up the phone and get a gardener no doubt.

He cannot clean his house - that is too much for him,

So, you pick up a phone and get a cleaner in.

He cannot cook his own food anymore,

So, you get on the internet and find chefs galore.

Then when it comes to his personal care,

You can pay for a qualified nurse to be there.

So, with the gardening and cooking and the cleaning done,

With nurses coming in to care for your loved one,

No form filling or begging or going to board,

For something that those with money can easily afford.

For me the answer is the system and this I would change,

It's the system we need to re arrange,

I would pay unpaid carers the same as the agency,

Not the weekly carers allowance of sixty-seven pounds fifty.

You see at twenty or thirty pounds per hour, the agency rate,

Financially, life for unpaid carers would be great,

They would have no form filling or begging to do,

They would have time to care for the disabled too,

They could get them things that they so need,

They could even get a mortgage indeed!

They could also pay someone that minimum wage, so they get a break,

Not taxing carers that would be great!

But unless you have been there,

Financially struggling whilst you care.

You will have no idea what goes on,

And how some of us have to be so strong,

They say Money can't buy happiness and maybe that is

right,

But redistributing it would aid unpaid carers, the disabled

and their plight.

50 Miles Away

In his flat, 50 miles away,

I speak to him almost every day,

And I track him on his phone,

He knows I'm with him so he's not alone.

He worries me senseless with out-of-date food,

And when he hasn't eaten, he's in a terrible mood,

Oh, his fridge is full to the brim,

But what's he eating? So, I worry over him.

He is 86 years old, don't you know,

Better social life than me! Always on the go!

And he has a companion who lives upstairs,

She is lovely and she really cares.

Living far away,

I worry about him every day,

So I call him up on Face-time on his phone,

Waiting patiently, I don't see him, but can hear him moan.

"You there? Where are you?', I quickly utter,

As I see his bedroom full of clutter,

'Dad, can you see me?" I quickly ask,

Face-time calling is no easy task,

'Nope' he says, 'why can't I?'

'Where are you? Nope, that's a fly',

Oh yes, I got the fly, the tv and the floor,

But not the man I was making the facetime call for.

But eventually I could see he was ok,

He found me this time today,

Social media just isn't his thing,

All the technology this day and age does bring.

Later that evening, a phone call came my way,

'Daughter dearest can you help me today?

I've dropped me phone on my naked body,

Taken a pic and it's gone you see.'

'Are you naked again?' I quickly ask,

'Yep, and I've accidentally taken a picture of me arse',

So I search the net to quickly find,

A picture of all his mankind!

But it's ok, it's only a knee,

And not his masculinity!

Dad, please put your clothes on when you are at home,

His reply 'I'm 86 and I'm alone',

'Sod it', he says 'I'm ok,

Thanks for all you have done today'.

I am grateful as he has friends around,

That keep his feet firmly on the ground,

But caring for someone miles away,

Is really not easy I have to say.

Caring For A Child With Hidden Disabilities

When it comes to care of a child the authorities say,

Does your child need more care than another the same age

per se?

If not then help is not yours just yet,

You have to wait until they get,

To a stage where their disability is distinctive against

others,

Never mind the concerns of their dads and mothers.

Ah! but, your child may go to hospital more,

Than an able child of three or four,

The authorities say your child does not need more care,

As a parent you still have to be there.

So, what warrants more

care in their eyes?

Does the look of disability

have to be their demise?

Now I have seen kids with disabilities far and wide,

I have one myself and she gives me such pride,

She has grown up now,

But her disabilities have somehow,

Made her into the woman she is today,

But we had to fight hard for help along the way.

As a child her disabilities were hidden,

And we had to fight for everything we were given,

But the one question that came back at every stage,

How is she different to others her age?

The endless forms you have to fill in,

I tell you, you want to reach for the gin!

The ins and out of a gnat's arse,

Attaining DLA was such a farce,

Unless when looking at your child others could see,

That the child clearly had an obvious disability.

There are the kiddies who depend on a wheelchair,

Where authorities could clearly see they needed care,

Ideologically, their tick boxes could be filled out more
easily,

Compared to a child with ADHD,

Or Type one diabetes or dyslexia,

Or dyscalculia or dyspraxia,

There are many more conditions on the list,

But wanted you to get the gist.

In order to get financial help or any kind of aid,

You have to prove how their disability affects them, in
order to get paid.

Now when your ADHD child is hanging off of a roof,

Or they have just tripped over and broken another tooth,

Or your dyslexic child is
frustrated as hell,

Or your child who needs extra care is not doing so well,

To then have to beg for the help they need,

Is stressful, stressful indeed.

In this day and age, it should just take,

A letter of diagnosis from a doctor for heaven's sake.

It's obvious that a child with ADHD and or dyslexia,

Is going to need a bit more care,

Or a child with type one diabetes or epilepsy,

Is going to need more day-to-day energy.

But the 50-page forms you have to fill out,

Is just added stress that authorities bring about.

As for the teachers that look after these children,

There is no doubt that some of them,

Are brilliant and know just what to do,

When your child needs an extra hand or two.

Then those who say it's not their job to do extra care,

For your child as they are not a nurse but a teach-er!

So, on top of caring for your child with disabilities,

The daily issues that arise from the authorities,

Really do not help or ease your woes,

In fact, they add to them all the way you go.

Then one day you get a call,

You are entitled to help after all,

But your battle may take you several years,

Of sheer blood, sweat and loads of tears.

Not to mention some parts of society,

Who look at you and just cannot see,

What you are dealing with every day,

Benefit scroungers you hear them say.

Or that little sod next door is on the roof,

And you think crikey if only you experienced the truth,

It's not bad parenting or scrounging that got me here,

It's the love of someone different that I hold very dear.

My life is a battle
all the time,

From looking after
this special child
of mine.

Not to mention
the rest of the family,
They are all effected too you see,
Because everything planned can go wrong,
And they are suddenly singing a different song,
Their world is tipped upside down as well,
And they can live a living hell.

Their childhood overtaken by their sister or brother,
And their needs are like no other,
You see they can get labelled too,
And they also have extra work to do,
So just because a child does not look disabled or poorly in
any way,
Does not mean they do not need extra care every day!

The Little Brown Envelope

Every unpaid carer knows there is a job to dread,

It's the one that spins and spins in my head,

It's the dreaded
brown envelope
that comes
through the
door,

The one that
wants to know
all about who
you are caring
for.

Why is this little form such a nuisance you ask,

Well, it isn't little! IT'S A HUGE RUDDY TASK!!!!

Not only that but one word you forget to write there,

Gives a different meaning to what is needed for care,

Now, it is not only carers who fill these forms out,

Also, some disabled people of that there is no doubt.

Therefore, the questions are not asked about what care is given,

But how the disabled and their daily lives, of disability is driven.

So, I would like to imagine just for a minute,

Whilst you are sat there with your coffee and biscuit,

Ernie and his unpaid carer with the form on their laps,

Trying to explain to those benefit Chaps,

What Ernie's life is and how it has become,

By answering a few questions, here is number one:

It asks for name, address and phone number,

You smile at each other as this you remember,

And then as you flick the page you see,

Another page that is quite easy.

This time a professional who knows you well,

Ah that's Dr Brown and now you are feeling swell,

Dr Brown's number, you know it off the top of your head,

You have dialled it so often, in your mind it is embed,

And his address, you know that for sure,

You have been there this week three times or four,

'I have got this', you both think as you jump with joy,

But turn the page and you think, 'Oh Boy'.

This is where an easy question at first,

Starts to cause your head, your head, to burst,

Tell us about the help you need,

You stare at the question that is easy to read.

Help I need? Where to start?

Don't worry the good old DWP have broken the questions
apart!

Oh yes, so here we go,

Big breath - we will still be writing this tomorrow!

Question One - Help you need when having a bath,

Ernie says, 'Would they like me to draw a graph?

'I need help with getting undressed and hoisting in,

Testing the water and washing me ding-aling'.

Oh and how many times day,

Do you need help in this way?

Twice for the

reply you put

two in the

square,

'And how long

each time do you

need this care?'

'How long each time? I do not count the minutes,

I am too busy trying not to push my limits!

I will leave this for later and ask my carer to watch the

clock,

Ask her how long it takes to wash me cock!

So now you turn to Question Two,

'Do you need help going to the loo?

And if so, what help do you need?

Tell us what help you need for a wee,'

Well, the questions about every nook and cranny,

They come thick and fast from head to your fanny,

Then comes the one, 'do you need someone awake with you

at night?'

Yep, but now them hands are too sore to write,

You now have writer's cramp from filling this form,

And this my friends is the norm!

So us carers toddle off to make a another cup of tea,

And give our hands a rest for an hour or three,

It's not just your hands your back it does ache,

From writing all this info for goodness sake!

Well, over your drink you stare at the logo DWP,

And things blur into eternity,

You see, whilst you are filling out this paperwork,

The powers that be forget that you work!

By now the person you

care for suddenly

needs you to do other

things,

Like getting their

dinner and all that

caring brings.

It may be a day or two before you can restart,

This form where you have to pour out your heart,

The questions are endless and all the same,

Do the DWP think you enjoy this game?

Well eventually to the form you return,

And wonder how much more you can write before you get

the burn?

Getting around is the question when you know you are nearly there,

You have finished the bit on personal care!

How many metres can you walk unaided? is the next they want to know,

And do you walk fast or really slow?

You have spent the past two days filling out this crap,

You have told them about the daytime nap,

You told them about falling over when getting dressed,

And you told them for carers help you are heaven blessed.

By now, you would think the DWP would know the norm,

That them named 'ere upon the form,

Cannot walk without holding someone's hand,

And here carers are trying to get them to understand.

Why does it have to be repeated for them to comprehend,

That on a wheelchair they depend,

They now repeat themselves and ask again,

Leaving the disabled and carers in frustrated pain!

But finally, you finish repeating yourself over and over,

The form is filled out and you are in clover,

BUT you still can't take a rest for a bit,

Because now the evidence you must hit!

Yep, now you have to sift through letters galore,

To prove that disability lives the other side of your door,

They don't want the endless outpatient letters you have in your hand,

They want diagnosis letters as they are grand.

Now, I don't know about you but it's clear to me,

That if you are diagnosed with Downs Syndrome you have a disability,

And what about Dementia and Cancer and Cerebral palsy
to name a few,
Wouldn't the diagnosis alone give the DWP a clue?

That there may be a struggle with day-to-day life,
So why do they cause so much strife?

Eventually all the evidence is collated,
And that form for days you berated,
Can finally go in the post,
You have done your upmost,
You are knackered and shattered and all written out,
You carried on caring for that there is no doubt.

That form that caused you so much stress,
Is now sat upon someone's desk,
And whilst you wait to see if you filled it out right,
You toss and turn and don't sleep at night.

The household income is in someone else's domain,
Will you get DLA or PIP again?

You hear the DWP are turning everyone down,

So, for the next few weeks you wear a frown.

People who know you say you will be fine,

But you are already living on the breadline,

And your stomach churns as the brown envelope comes through the door,

That's the outcome of the form for sure!

Now my friends I would like to say that you open the letter to find,

The DWP have awarded something and been kind,

But too many times, the disabled are awarded nowt,

The DWP are making them go without!

Every day for them is a fight to stay alive,

And they depend on DWP in order to strive,

And you only need someone who does not understand what you write,

To put the household into a dire plight.

You see without PIP or DLA,

The unpaid carers get no pay!

Yep, I wonder how many of you realise,

That without PIP or DLA they also meet their demise.

And so you have someone disabled with no care,

No one to wash or brush their hair,

No one to get them dressed and fed,

And so the disabled can end up dead!

The PIP and DLA form is so important to get right,

It's a lifeline for the disabled, their carers and their fight,

So next time you hear someone is at home all day,

Living on your taxes whilst you have to work away,

Remember they are working all night through,

Trying to keep someone alive is all they can do.

As for the forms

that come through

the post,

The government are

doing what they hate most,

Paying money for someone to see,

What it's like to live with a disability,

For the DWP I would save some money if I was you,

And go on pure diagnosis for a decade or two.

One letter from the doctor is all you need,

To prove you are disabled and disabled indeed.

As for carers that work for less than two pounds an hour,

We are holding up this shambolic shower,

And we know that when that brown envelope drops

through the door,

That DWP could be asking us to give some more.

They could be sending us to appeal,

Just so we have some money for a meal,

So the disabled and carers,

Feel like beggars,

And that should not be,

Not in the 21st century.

For those who get up everyday and for an employer they

work,

And think caring is a job shirk,

Please swap your job with a carer for a week,

Fill out the forms that make us so meek,

At the same time, keep someone else alive that you will care for,

Then you will realise the importance of the brown envelope that drops through the door.

Where Do Kids In Wheelchairs Play?

Where do kids in

wheelchairs play?

When they ask, "Can

I go to the park

today?"

You know that deep in your heart,

Going to the park will tear you apart.

Where do kids in Wheelchairs play?

When they ask, "Can I go to the park today?"

And the tears you hide,

When they ask to go onto the slide.

Where do kids in Wheelchairs play?

When they ask, "Can I go to the park today?"

And the many tears that they bring,

When they ask to go on a swing.

Where do kids in Wheelchairs play?

When they ask, "Can I go to the park today?"

And there is no hiding your doubt,

When they ask to go on the roundabout.

Where do kids in Wheelchairs play?

When they ask, "Can I go to the park today?"

And you may want someone to blame,

When they ask to go on the climbing frame.

Where do kids in Wheelchairs play?

When they ask "Can I go to the park today?"

Some Unpaid Carers Know

Some unpaid carers know this,

Some unpaid carers don't,

Some unpaid carers will apply for this,

Some unpaid carers won't.

The government have

said unpaid carers

need a break,

So, with social

services another form

you undertake.

We will call this a carers assessment,

To see how they are coping on their anti-depressant!

Oh yes, it appears,

That with caring hope disappears,

And whilst I thought it was only me,

It appears it's a large amount of our caring family!

Anti-depressants, something we do not have to fight for,

Oh, you are caring, you need these for sure,

You say, 'actually doc I need something more,

Than what these anti-depressants are prescribed for.

The doc refers you to social services and out they come,

To talk to you about your dad or your mum,

Or your daughter or son,

'Would you like us to put them into care?'

"No I bloody don't, that's not fair!"

'How can we help?' They say with that questioning look,

For a start, supply us a carer who can read a book,

Someone to help with common sense,

Send someone whose skills are not a pretence'.

'I cannot do that', they hurriedly say,

'But this is what I can do for you today,

I can give you some money that is just for you,

But first, we have to fill in a form or two!'

'A bloody
form, not
again,
Is it
worth it
to keep
me sane?

If I fill out that form, what will I get?' you ask,
'Because I am sorry, it is just another task,
And us carers have so much to do,
We don't want to fill out a form or two.'

'Ah, but you need this' they say,
'This will take you on holiday!'
'A holiday? Really?' You squeal,
Oh yes, the bliss, you really start to feel,

The sun on your

face,

That ocean air,

And you can

have this

because you

care?

You have no money to go away,

'So, this is worth it' you hurriedly say,

'Yes, I will fill in your form on how I cope,

And a holiday for me, yes there's hope'.

Then you sit over a cuppa for an hour or so,

Then social services say, 'I have to go,

But I will see what I can do,

To get you a bob or two'.

Then you ask, 'how much can I get?',

And they say, '£300 for that sunset'.

'£300 what will I do with that,

That only covers the boarding of the cat.

That will not get me on a plane,

And I have just spent an hour going insane,

I have just spilled out my guts to you,

You have taken a way an hour or two!'

'I will see what I can do', they quietly reassure,

As they turn around and walk out the door.

Some are lucky and get the doe,

But it's not enough on holiday to go.

Some say be thankful you have it at all,

And it's this that makes many a carer fall,

We have to be thankful for what we get,

And yet,

Form filling and begging
seems how the system is
set.

How about just sending a £300 payment through?

To all unpaid carers every year or two?

With a note saying, 'For your caring we give thanks,

All unpaid carers have got this in their banks?'

So, yes my fellow carers you are entitled to a carers assessment,

But if filling out forms can be a form of resentment,

Then think before you rush to spill your guts on the floor,

Because a payment is not guaranteed for sure.

And if you are lucky to get something through,

There are restrictions on how you spend it too,

£300 can be given for a holiday,

But away from your loved ones you have to stay.

These days £300 does not get you very far,

I had one for a gym membership, but I needed a car,

As my nearest gym was miles away,

So, I couldn't use it anyway.

You have to remember these payments are for you,

In thanks for what you do,

But despite having no food in the fridge,

Or wanting to throw yourself off the bridge,

You cannot use it for food and bills,

Or so you can sit at night without any chills,

It's for you to do something nice,

It doesn't matter you can't afford a pack of rice.

No, this is your bonus to show they care,

But still wanting to control the money that for you is
there.

Every carer is different it's true,

So, if the carers assessment can really help you,

Then go for it and see what can be done,

But don't expect money for dad or for mum,

Or daughter or son.

You might be able to get other services though,

Something away from the £300 doe,

They may be able to send more help in,

It might be worth a chat, you may still win.

I say win, the wrong word I probably did use,

It is not there to confuse,

It is just us experienced carers know,

That form filling causes us so much woe,

And we get to the stage where we have to ask,

If this particular form will be worth the task.

For some carers it will,

For some carers it won't,

Some carers do,

And some carers don't.

Your Home Is Not Yours Anymore

What happens when sickness comes knocking at the door?

It's simple, your home is not yours anymore,

No more designer sofas and clean carpets are rare,

Instead you get a commode and a lovely wheelchair!

Then there's
the hoists
and the
hospital beds,

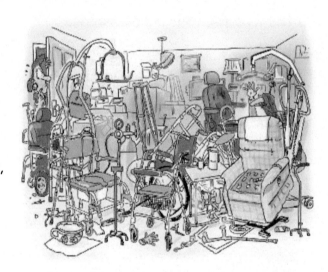

Oh yes, you have all this instead,

You sit there remembering the living room you once had,

The one that is now piled high with incontinence pads,

Not to mention the various machines,

That all comes with what sickness brings.

The 'Ross Returns' the elderly love them they do,

Stick me on there love and take me to the loo,

Now if you have not seen a Ross Return before,

You have a real treat in store!

These things are like trolleys that you stand on and hold,

When the legs do not do as they are told,

And you can stand and get wheeled to the loo,

Save the legs for that minute or two,

Now if the legs are really weak,

Then these machines may help the physique,

But if your mum is like mine,

To her this is play time!!

'Nope I'm not going to use my legs if I don't have to,

You can use that thing to take me to the loo,'

So, in the living room you have a wheelchair and commode,

And the Ross Return to take you down the road,

And the incontinence pads are evident,

Just in case you have an accident.

And if that's not enough your mates don't fit anymore,

Because they struggle to get in the front door

And then there's the smell,

We all know this one so well,

Air fresheners you put round the room,

And the 'shake n vac' and the good old vacuum,

But that does not get rid of the smell of that 'log'

Never mind you can blame it on the dog.

Some paid carers don't mind a bit,

If they have nowhere to sit,

They find a spot and they just stand,

Next to your cared for holding their hand.

And the carpets that are filthy dirty too,

But you just have so much surrounding you,

'Don't worry 'bout the carpets' paid carers say,

'They can wait for another day'.

So, you sit there amongst machines and pads and

equipment galore,

And your home is not your home anymore,

But your cared for has the best,

They are home in their own little nest,

They have the care money can't buy,

Just no space for you or I!

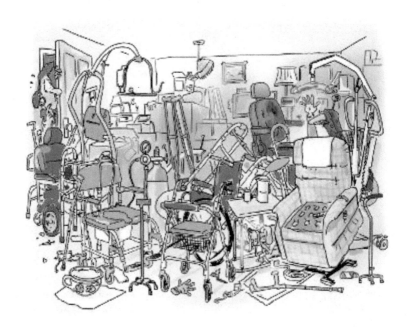

You Sit There!

When a carer comes over the door,

You know if you have a good one for sure,

Because in their vocabulary,

Are three little words they will say often to thee,

There is no doubt, you know that they really care,

When they utter the three words, 'you sit there'.

Oh joy to the ears of those words to many an unpaid

carer,

From someone who is everything from bottom washer to

hoover repairer,

Oh yes, they know what the hose on the hoover is for,

They know how to use a hoist unaided for sure,

And when you ask if they need help to wash your loved

one's hair,

They answer you back, 'No, you sit there'.

Oh yes, they also want to look after you,

To give you a break for that hour or two,

They are worth their weight in gold,

They are experienced and capable and do not need to be told,

They have come to show you they care,

And finally, you know you can just sit there!!

Caring For A Child Who Needs A Wheelchair

Caring for a child

who needs a

wheelchair,

Brings situations

that are hard to

bear,

Because their disability with it brings,

A whole host of difficult things,

From personal care and lack of mobility,

Their problems are clear for all to see.

You get the looks and the stare,

As you are in town with the wheelchair.

I say wheelchair as that is all some people see,

They don't see your child without the disability,

Or, they see the disability first and cannot help but stare,

At the four wheels that you are holding there.

But in the chair is someone you hold dear,

The child of yours has caused many a tear,

The child who at the age of eight,

For the first time stood up today nice and straight,

The tears you cried were that of sheer pride,

Eight years you waited and your child has tried and tried,

And today they did it, but strangers do not know,

They just stare at you with wheelchair in tow.

They have no idea at what you have been through,

To keep your child safe and next to you,

They smile at you as if to say,

I feel sorry for you in every kind of way.

Then they rush past you without a word from their lips,

But you know they are staring at the handlebars between

your hips.

Your little one thinks they are going to talk to them,

"Hello", they say but are ignored once again,

Then as the child grows and realises how much they are

ignored,

They know just what to do to keep from being so bored,

They beg you for a 'power-chair' to make it easier for you,

And you have no idea what they are about to do.

For when that 'power-chair' finally comes through the door,

They beg you to take them to the store,

As they take the
throttle in their hands,

It is now that you can
see just what they
have planned,

Oh yes, it's payback for all the times you fell over me,
Or pretended that you just didn't see,
Because in a wheelchair you can be a sitting duck,
For people may treat you like a piece of muck.

To treat you as if you are indifferent to those who can walk,
Indifferent to those who are lucky enough to be able to talk,

But with that throttle held tightly in their hand,

It's payback time for them who think they are so grand,

The child in the wheelchair is suddenly powered,

They no longer feel like a coward.

With thoughts and speech running through their brain,

They know they won't feel like that again,

They look at you and you know what their thoughts are,

The one in the wheelchair may as well be in a car!

Because now they are powered and you know them so well,

These are the thoughts in their brain for me to tell,

Fall over me today and just watch what I will do,

Because now - ha ha - I can run over you!

And you watch them strangers run, duck and dive,

Whilst they say, "sorry, its new, I don't know how to

drive".

And watch people's faces when they see they have a brain,
I promise you my dears you will never ignore someone in a
wheelchair again!

The Culture Barrier

Whether you are Sri Lankan, British or Italian,

French, German or African,

Or from anywhere in the world,

Too many to list and to unfold,

Our cultures are different in many a way,

And is seen in how we live from day-to-day.

Culture Barriers that may not normally be there,

Can be strikingly obvious in the world of care.

At first, I questioned if it was personality or the culture

we had,

That caused a barrier that made us sad.

We have had many carers of different cultures come to
look after us,

Some were fab and made no fuss,

Others were more, 'I'm not doing that',

'What clear up after your dog or cat?'

Was it their culture or upbringing or training I had to ask,

When they were so clearly not doing a task?

I questioned the carers who are always late,

Was it their upbringing that sealed their fate?

But very often these carers treated you as their family,

Mum, dad, brother and Great Auntie.

There are carers who were on time for eternity,

But, this caused problems in emergencies,

Because they couldn't stay, they had to go,

To be on time for next client, Flo,

Overtime you notice a correlation between culture and
behaviour,

And so you have a dilemma to savour.

What do you do when a carer cannot understand a word
you say,
But they are there to help you today?

What about carers who speak too sharp or far too quick?
But are still there to help those wounds you lick,
There are them who have been brought up to look after
nan,
So it is natural for them to help intimately where they
can.

But they are like this with other clients too,
And over time their caring of others means they are late
for you.

Now it would be so fab and so great,
If you had one carer with all of the good traits,
But alas carers are usually good at one thing,
And we found that often it was down to their culture and
upbringing.

Some are good all-rounders but have a clear broken accent,

But the cared for have no idea 'what they just meant'.

So, I hear you say what is their crime,

If they fail to turn up on time?

Or if they are not fluent in your language,

Is this really to be regarded as unwanted baggage?

Well, um, yes, it is when they need mum on her feet,

And another language is all they can tweet,

So, your mum who only speaks English,

Gets a long line of words that are Polish,

Or Nigerian or French all of which she hasn't a clue,

And they are trying to get her out of a pad of poo,

Or your mum or dad may only know French or Italian,

And they get the English with their broad English Tongue!

Now I am English and I can cook,

I can easily read an English cookery book,

BUT, if that cookery book is in another language or two,

I wouldn't have a fig of what to do!

I cannot speak anything other than English,

So, I could not verbalise with someone who speaks only

Polish,

And imagine if you had lost the ability to gesture,

And you were the one who needed care?

Would you not need someone,

Who had the same mother tongue?

Or, if for some reason you have lost your sight,

Wouldn't you find that the language difference is a huge

blight?

People all over the world have come to you in your time of

need,

They are lovely people, lovely indeed,

But people are brought up in different ways,

And are taught different priorities and different cliches.

This culture barrier in care really needs a review,

Not just for the families and cared for, but paid carers

too.

The paid carers are dealing with every kind of disability,

From people who are not able to hear or see,

To dementia sufferers who may understand differently.

Then add to the culture difference, personalities and
attitude,

From what one culture considers to be rude,

Another may have been brought up this way,

And whilst different cultures are living side by side in
Britain today,

When it comes to the care of someone of a different
culture or nationality,

Should we not consider the barriers of cultural
reasonability?

Mums Who Sleep All Day

Have you got a mum who sleeps all day?

But when you go up to her and say,

'Would you like a
nice cup of tea?'

She opens one
eye so she can
see.

Now it's just one eye that opens you understand,

Opening two would mean you have the upper hand,

Because that would mean you know she's awake,

And that means sleeping she can no longer fake!

Oh yes, they can get crafty our old peeps,

And make out they are fast asleeps,

When truth is they just can't be bothered to talk to you,

So, they make out they're asleep, that's what they do!

But when you offer them something they find nice,

Them peepers they are open in a trice,

First the one eye looks at you,

If you're telling the truth they open two!!

Oh Chocolate biscuits or a piece of cake,

Mention M and S and they're wide awake!

Yep, not only awake but sitting up as well,

'Oh I like M and S they are swell'.

But you go in and say it's meds time now,

You have no hope she turns into a right lickle cow!

'Mum, wakey
wakey, the doc
wants you to take
these',

And you do your level best to appease,

You just know them eyes are going to stay shut,

And you have this feeling deep down in your gut.

You tell her she can take them with an alcoholic drink,

Then you see them eyes twitching whilst she has a think,

Then one eye opens but no drinkie poos around,

So, she shuts it quickly without making a sound.

Then there are the guests for whom she doesn't care,

She stays asleep the entire time they are there,

The minute she knows that they have gone,

Them eyes are open cause she was awake all along.

'Why didn't you speak to your guests mummy dear?',

'Don't have to - I don't want them here',

The same happens on the hospital ward,

I'm sure there's a book explaining this accord.

I have seen it with my very own eyes,

All ten patients asleep was a mere disguise,

The minute you offered them a treat,

Them eyes would open in a heartbeat.

So, if your elderly loved one is sleeping too,

It could just be they don't want to talk to you!!

Time

Time, where does it go?

Tick Tock, Tick Tock,

No time to show.

The Milk

There was an unpaid carer called Nikki,

Who asked her carer called Ricky,

To bring her four pints of milk,

Instead, she got silk,

Now, that's just taking the Mickey.

She Arrived Yesterday

She locked herself
out for the third
time that day,

The live in carer
who arrived
yesterday,

She also forgot to
feed and water
mum,

Needless to say her
time was soon done.

My Mate Jeff

'What's it like to be deaf?',

I signed to my mate called Jeff,

'No idea' he said to me,

'I hear with my eyes through which I see'.

What Is A Type-One?

What is a type one?

I asked my mum?

At the age of six,

With needles and finger pricks.

"It's where your body doesn't produce Insulin" she said,

"We have to put it in artificially instead",

And for that we have cried and cried,

But we are thankful that I never died.

Charles Bonnet

Charles Bonnet is something new,

That has misguided a doctor or two,

You see with this, confusion and hallucinations appear,

And to them this is dementia, this is clear,

But it's not, it's an eyesight issue,

Misdiagnosed with dementia - who ever knew?

And Mother Makes Four

So they don't feel so alone,

You may fight to get your loved one into a care home,

Let's face it you have tried all the agencies in town,

And all they have done is left you with a frown.

A care home appears your only way,

Of getting through each and every day,

You cry for the next

decade,

Feeling guilty that care

is not your 'homemade'.

You have life to live,

And love to give,

A partner to feed,

And children in need.

And now, you are about
to become skint even
more,
When care home fees
come knocking at your
door!

But after pulling your hair out doing this caring thing,
You don't care anymore about the purse string!

You have pleased the kids and your husband, Laurence,
And you can go visit mum, but then you find 'Florence',
Florence is not your mum, but is in mum's room,
Sweeping the floor with a broom.

'Hello' you gingerly say,
'Are you the cleaner today?'
Your mum is sat in the chair,
Shaking her head at Florence who is unaware,
Then you realise that Florence is a resident,
And that her struggle with dementia is evident.

Well, she sweeps round the chair that your mum is sat in,

And hits mums' legs as she does her cleaning,

There is no nurse or carer in sight,

Just your mum and Florence hitting her with all her might,

You sit there not having a clue,

You once had just your mum, now you have two!

Then Dave enters fiddling with his trouser string,

Not only that but also his 'thing',

And you look at your mum who clearly knows these two,

And she says, 'watch him, he's about to do a Poo!'

Well, as the trousers come down and he tries to squat,

I found I was helping him to use the pot,

I hit the bell as I now have three,

Dementia residents surrounding me.

Before help arrives, Joan has joined in the fun,

Rifling through the wardrobe that belongs to mum,

I sat there dazed as I now had four,

And I prayed and hoped, there were no fucking more!

Joan scratched her head as she tries to find,

Skirts, trousers and tops of her kind.

The nurse finally arrives asking, 'what is going on in here?

You shouldn't be looking after all of them my dear,

Come with me', she says to Florence, 'come this way,

There is a singer in the lounge today!'

'What about the other two?

Can you not take them with you?'

But the nurse is already out of the door,

But you sigh with relief that you no longer have four!

A little while later a carer hands mum a plate,

Two grapes and a minuscule piece of cake,

And I mean minuscule like your small fingernail,

And yep, just TWO grapes for one so frail.

As the carer walks out the door,

Joan and Dave see the treats in store,

And yes, you guessed just what happened next,

They nicked the two grapes, leaving mum perplexed!

Mum's hand moved so fast as you can believe,

To ensure the cake was hers indeed,

This was mum's afternoon tea,

And it was shared between the three.

Very often I would have a call to say,

Mum has fallen out of bed today,

Or 'mum has a bruise and we do not know how,

Must have hit her head on the wall somehow'.

But, you've seen Florence, Gladys and Dave down the hall,

Fighting with each other and having a brawl,

With no carers or nurses to be found,

The residents' families are now referee and mediator

bound!

Oh yes, Dave shouting, with sleeves rolled up and fists in the air,

Saying, 'Come and take me on, if you dare',

Then, Gladys yells, 'you don't want to fight with me,

My son's the boxer, Mohammed Ali!'

Florence, is in amongst it all with her broom,

Saying 'Fuck off you two, I need to clean this room!'

Oh yes, I saw it all,

Including Dave rifling through mum's knicker drawer,

'Where are they' he angrily stuttered,

'If only I had my pliers', he muttered,

'Blast it, they are not in there',

Carrying on cursing, 'darn it I have lost them somewhere'.

I glared at Dave, who had mum's smalls in his hand,

'I found these' he said, 'they will do just grand',

With that he walked out the door,

I wondered what he was going to use mum's knickers for,

Then I watched as he fell to his knees,

And tried to undo the plug in the hall if you please.

The upside to mum's nursing home were the singers I have

to say,

They brought normality to the everyday,

But I struggled with this environment,

And mum was really not that content,

So I got her out and home with me,

And looked after just her and not the other three!

The Cost Of Living

What does it cost to be disabled?

What does it cost to Care?

I hear you saying, what does it matter?

With all that money you have there,

You get benefits that help you galore,

That is what the benefit is for.

So, what happens when electricity prices soar,

When your shopping bill has trebled,

When the price of petrol costs a little bit more?

'Why are we any different to others?' you may ask,

'We are all in this together',

So tightening our belts has to be the task.

So tell me, how do you cut the use of a stairlift?

That needs to take you to bed?

How do you cut the cost of gluten-free food,

When a coeliac and type one diabetic needs to be fed?

And before you say, 'Ah but you get it on prescription',

It is a postcode lottery so to some that is pure fiction,

Some gluten-free food is already triple the price,

Paying for non gluten free food would be nice,

Because a tub of gravy granules is just a pound today,

But if you are coeliac THREE TIMES is what you will pay.

So, their food was already at an all-time high,

Added to this the cost of living,

A lot of coeliacs are struggling and you can see why.

How do you cut the cost of electrical equipment?

That is needed for chronic pain,

How do you cut the cost of charging a power chair?

Maybe you don't use these items again?

How do you cut the cost of a Watch that tells you when to breathe?

How do you cut down your travelling,

When it's to hospital appointments you seethe?

I hear some say, 'but this is paid, you can claim these things back',

You can if it's an NHS appointment,

Yes, they keep this on track,

BUT what if the NHS do not cover this type of care?

What happens then? How do you afford to get there?

Do you give up the things that help you well again?

Do you cut the cost of things that stop you going insane?

How do you cut the cost of equipment that keeps someone alive?

Just what part of their care should take that nose-dive?

Should you stop the appointments that keep them out of pain?

Or should you just not use the stairlift and not go to bed again?

Maybe you should eat food that is cheap but makes you sick?

Or turn off the devices that makes your struggling heart tick?

The gas usage was already cut down many years ago,

They already have got their energy bills low,

The water that is easy, they already share their bath,

Yep, that is sorted as they have already taken this path.

These are just some of the choices the disabled have to bear,

Not only the disabled, but the people who chose to care.

I cannot deliver the answers,

I cannot say do this,

But interaction from the government,

Would certainly not go amiss.

The Wage Couldn't Be Fairer

When we first started having agencies at our door,

They did everything in the care plan and some more,

They not only looked after the one that needed care,

They also looked after the knackered unpaid carers sat

there.

But overtime carers and social workers come and go,

And the system and new people started leaving me full of

woe,

I have now come to question the government authority,

On just what they will pay for, for the cared for and me.

Looking on the internet I became reassured,

That I wasn't going crazy at what was causing me to be

floored,

I now could clearly see,

That it wasn't just me!

BUT across the country it could be said to be true,

That the authorities are dictating to you!

They tell you what to pay a carer,

Saying the wage 'couldn't be fairer'.

But it is an insult,

And what you get as a result,

Is no care!

No-one there!

When I questioned the pay, the authorities said 'we can't be fairer',

For the money on offer, you can get a good carer!

But authorities in their office, do not appear to have a clue,

How difficult it is to get someone experienced on that pay to come and work for you.

So, fellow unpaid carers and them with a disability,

Is it the same in your vicinity?

When you say,

I cannot get anyone to do the work on that pay,

The authorities tell you to advertise,

But they just do not realise,

That the pay is an insult to many a paid carer,

 And adds salt to the wound by saying, 'we can't be fairer'.

Paid carers will not come and work for you,

When they see what they are expected to do,

You only have to see the internet,

To see the comments for what you get.

Whoever you employ will have great responsibility,

Looking after the person with a disability,

They may have to know how to change a canula,

Or change that bag called a stoma,

Or they may have to oversee medication galore,

And know what all those meds are for.

They have to ensure someone is watered and fed,

And know and be able to turn people safely in bed,

They have to know how to keep the cared for safe and sound,

To be the main carer when unpaid carers are not around.

They have to know how to operate,

Everything from hoists to the rickety front gate,

They may have to assist them into a car,

Because the cared for may not be able walk that far.

Not to mention the house has to be looked after too,

From dusting and polishing to cleaning the loo,

Ensuring that everything around is so much fresher,

All whilst keeping calm under pressure.

And then to be able to use a computer and to write,

Everything that they have done day and night,

So, when potential carers see ten pounds an hour,

They say, 'Sod off, you shambolic shower!'

And, I have seen many potential carers go underneath internet adverts,

Saying this, (and it really hurts),

You are offering such a low wage for all this,

You are just taking the piss!

But who puts the disabled into this position in the first place?

It's the authorities and it is a disgrace,

That they, who think they cannot be fairer,

Are making things so much worse for the disabled and the unpaid carer!

The Frustrated Carer

An unpaid carer I love to be,

If I wasn't dealing with hypocrisy.

The government hailing us as an unpaid hero,

When their financial regard is almost ZERO!

I have learnt most of the best carers out there,

Are those who offer the unpaid care.

And the love and commitment to the people they care for,

Gets little support from the system set by those in

Whitehall.

And so, I write my final poem for you,

I've gone mad I haven't a clue,

Everyone trying to take control,

Whilst unpaid carers sink further   and further

        into a hole.

Your blood pressure is
through the roof,

You have yet another
broken tooth,

Your glasses have
vanished into mid- air,

No time or money to
fix this as you care.

You have someone sick trying to cope,
And you're trying to give them hope,
So, you do what they need, that comes first,
Never mind quenching your thirst.

Other than caring,
You are information sharing,
Somewhere along the way,
You - yes you - you turn into decay.

The cared for is being looked after alright,

Whilst you just don't sleep at night,

You are knackered, shattered and totally worn out,

Always someone wanting an answer no doubt.

Many different agencies,

Care plans that bring you to your knees,

The constant calling of the GPs,

The receptionists and the pharmacies!

If it's not the cared for it's the paid caregivers,

You hold the answers and it gives you the shivers,

You don't have energy for the simple questions anymore,

Like what's this part of the hoover for?

You kidding Me? That's for the stairs,

You say to the carer in despair!

The new carer you have this week isn't doing so well,

Hopefully the new carer next week will be swell,

But, you rarely know who comes through the door,

Or if they are trained in anyway at all!

Your house, your
home is filled
with a different
face,

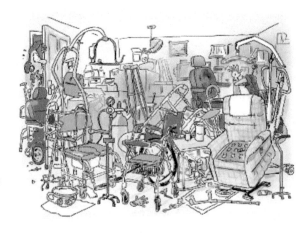

Your home is now
a working space.

Then you explode and say, 'sod off I can take no more,
When another untrained carer is knocking at your door!
You end up saying it is easier on my own,
Get out of my frigging home.

The dust will have to gather,
So, I don't get myself into a lather,
But getting mum to the loo,
There's a problem, what shall I do.

So, you call the agency and another carer walks through
the door,
You think, give it another try, just one more!

You have one eye open, the other is not,

The paid carer says, 'I have no not got',

What do you mean, have no not got? You quickly think,

This language barrier should be extinct,

'No not got? No not got?', what are they on about now?

Then you realise that mum somehow,

Is sat on the floor looking at you,

Carer says, 'it not just me, need two',

Oh, I just want to sleep, that is why you are here,

Can you not get on with the job my dear?

Busy is an understatement of people always wanting you,

They really think you have nothing to do!

And whilst I guess I have highlighted elderly care,

From speaking with others, I know that this happens

everywhere,

Whether caring for an adult, a teenager or child,

Caring is not a job for those who are mild,

It's frustrating, debilitating and so much more,

Sometimes I just sit and stare at the floor.

Other times I sit and stare at the TV,

That is one thing that wants nothing from me,

It is the one device that helps me get through,

I can take myself away for a minute or two.

And so yes folks, us carers are really stressed,

With having to get someone up, washed and dressed,

Not to mention medicated and fed,

Ensuring that they are alive and not dead.

Or stopping them from roaming far away,

Or stealing Elsie's Necklace today,

Or caring for a child who has special needs,

Who makes you count 1000 beads.

There are too many scenarios for me to state,

Caring gives you a huge amount upon your plate!

No parties or outings or new clothes

for you,

Life is about caring - that is all you

do!

So eventually we get depressed, very, very, depressed,

You eventually don't even get dressed,

It is part and parcel of the job,

And can lead you to have an almighty gob!

You laugh, shout and have a cry,

At times you are so tired you want to die.

You deal with professionals in care every day,

Whose misunderstanding of you leaves things in disarray,

They follow a set of rules,

That does not give them the in-between tools,

They have to learn you and that takes weeks,

For them to know everything from meds to sheets.

They do not lead your life it is true,

They don't know the household the way unpaid carers do,

The disabled, trying to find the right carer for them,

Is like a singleton trying to find her prince charming.

You speak with Sheila and Frances and Stanley too,

Loads of Agencies who promise to be there for you,

But like local authorities and CHC,

They all have these rules to follow you see.

Many of the rules lack consideration,

Are without Common sense and differentiation,

And people really try to help they do,

But half the time they haven't a clue.

The rules and red tape and procedures to follow,

Do not help you today or even tomorrow,

Unpaid carers are frustrated for sure,

Dealing with all these rules and red tape at their door.

Authorities saying no you cannot use money for that,

Overriding consultants and turning you down flat,

No-one wanting to help or taking responsibility,

A lot of times saying, 'that is not my job you see'.

Finances for most unpaid carers are at an all-time low,

We cannot financially help the disabled out of their

sorrow,

The government will give thousands to agencies galore,

But leave the unpaid carers destitute and poor.

How refreshing would it be,

For the government to say you can claim like an agency?

We would not have to beg for things that we need.

Because for 24-hour care of agency pay,

Unpaid carers could buy things for their cared for today.

With that we could get a mortgage,

For housing then there would be a bridge.

We could buy the adaptions they need just to live,

Without begging agencies what they have to give?

We could do so much with this wage,

So government think whilst you are reading this page,

And professionals please I am begging you don't make an

error,

You are probably dealing with a ......

knackered,

haggard,

poor……. broke……..

    destitute,

FRUSTRATED CARER!!

About the Author

Brianne George is a new writer to the publishing world, but comes with ample experience in writing, having written poetry and keeping friends and family entertained with it since her teens.

Brianne graduated with a Master's in creative Writing in 2005 and is now putting the techniques she learnt into practice.

Her writing comes from her experience in the world, having been an unpaid carer to her mum and daughter for many years.

She now lives in South of England with her disabled daughter and dog. You will often find her with a chocolate bar in her hand and if you find her out of her pj's and with brushed hair you know it's a special occasion!

Brianne hopes that her book will resinate with the many unpaid carers out there, but also, will highlight the changes that are so desperately needed to be made to make a difference.

Having been pushed by friends and family, Brianne has finally taken the leap to turn her work into a published book for you all to read.

Phone Numbers of Organisations to Contact for Help

Carers Uk   0808 808 7777

Carers Trust   0300 772 9600

Scope   0808 800 3333

Age UK   0800 678 1602

Action for
Carers Surrey   0303 040 1234

THE FRUSTRATED CARER

FRUSTRATED AGAIN!!

BY

BRIANNE GEORGE

Illustrated by John Elson

Printed in Great Britain
by Amazon

82177832R00099